The Punniest Joke Book
The Ultimate Collection of Puntastic Gags
By Chester Croker

One Liner Jokes

This huge collection of puntastic one liner jokes are sure to make you laugh out loud. This is quite simply the best collection of the very best punniest jokes you are likely to come across.

This one liner joke book contains five hundred punny jokes. You will find plenty of great one-liners, many wonderful word play gags, some quick fire puns and what are known as Dad jokes, all of which are designed to be easy to remember. Most of these one liner jokes are funny and some are very funny.

There is something for everyone and this huge collection of funny one liners is full of memorable puns and gags to make you laugh out loud, or snigger to yourself. All in all, this book is the puniest joke book ever and is simply guaranteed to have you in stitches.

Published by Glowworm Press
7 Nuffield Way
Abingdon OX14 1RL

FOREWORD

When I was approached to write a foreword to this book I was very flattered.

That is until I was told that I was the last resort by the author, Chester Croker, and that everyone else he had asked had said they couldn't do it!

I have known Chester for a number of years and his ability to create funny jokes is absolutely incredible.

He is quick witted and an expert at crafting clever puns and amusing gags and he will be glad you have bought this book, as he has an expensive lifestyle to maintain.

Enjoy!

Paige Turner

When I was young, I won the school trampolining championship - three years on the bounce.

I swallowed a camera this morning. I'm now experiencing flashbacks.

Does anyone know a cure for excessive ear wax? If you do, please give me a shout.

Why does a bottle of poison have a use by date?

Athlete's foot, if anything, has made me slower.

I'm half way towards my goal of becoming one of the idle rich.

Nobody seems to know what 'Je ne sais quoi' means.

I have joined a band called 999 Megabytes. We haven't got a Gig yet.

The police rang me earlier to say they'd recovered my stolen three piece suite. That was nice of them, it was starting to look a bit tatty.

My girlfriend wanted an animal skin coat. So I got her a donkey jacket.

I used to be addicted to the Hokey Cokey, but I turned myself around.

My barber has announced that he can't cut my hair any longer.

My uncle fought in the war and survived mustard gas and pepper spray. He is now called as a seasoned veteran.

I am recovering from an addiction to ice cream. I'm OK now but it's been a rocky road.

I intend to live forever. So far, so good.

My wife asked for something with diamonds in it for our wedding anniversary. I got her a pack of cards.

I'm moving to France to become a baker. After all, money baguettes money.

Did the guy who invented dominoes spot an opportunity?

My Aunt Marge is still sick. I can't believe she's still not butter.

I'm a hopeless businessman - my origami business has folded.

Yesterday I took the family to Oak Furniture Land. It has to be the worst theme park I've ever been to.

I hate it when people get all intellectual about Beethoven although they've never seen one of his paintings.

A mate of mine bragged about how much super glue he could eat. He now keeps his mouth shut.

Golden retrievers. I find them very fetching.

I've just been to a fisherman's disco. Lots of sole music.

I'm mourning the loss of my pet hamster. Tragically he died at the wheel.

Apparently there's an Arctic Circle lottery. You have to be inuit to win it.

I was offered a job as a grave digger recently. I turned it down as it's a dead end job.

I have a new job. I'm now a plastic surgeon. It's raised a few eyebrows.

My wife told me off for making a mess on the kitchen floor while I was making an omelette. I'm now walking around the house on egg shells.

I was in agony cooking beef tonight. It really was painstaking.

I hate my job working at the bridge. It's really taking its toll.

You are invited to a bird party. RSPB.

I have just bought a pen that writes underwater. The good news is that it writes other words too.

I lost my job working in a watch factory - they wanted someone with a more 'hands-on' approach.

I've quit my job working for Nike. Just couldn't do it anymore.

I've written a book on how to become an attorney. I think you'll like it. Judge for yourself.

I've got a new job making chess pieces. I start on knights next week.

My wife always mentions my naked wrist. I'd better keep a watch on it.

If someone copies a plague without permission, would that be plaguerism?

I like a woman who wears beads. You know you can count on her.

Explosion in Pi Factory. 3.1415927 Dead.

The Devon music festival has had to be cancelled after the organisers couldn't decide who should go on first – The Jam or The Cream.

My local fish and chips shop has been burgled. The plaice was turned over.

I have pet insurance, so I should get a courtesy cat while mine is at the vet.

I got a job in the prison library. It has its pros and cons.

I got sacked from the watch factory for spending too much time on my movements.

I used to be uncertain, but I'm not so sure now.

I took part in the sun tanning Olympics. I just got bronze.

I wonder if midgets start a story with, "When I was little."

Did anyone think to get Jack and Jill a Get Well Soon card?

In Stevie Wonder's song 'Superstition' how did he know the writing was on the wall?

I live in a Neighbourhood Watch area. Never seems to be my turn to wear it though.

My uncle did his National Service in the Black Forest, Germany. He said it was a piece of cake.

My wife and I have had an argument over how tight I am. She's now in the kitchen ripping all the plates in half.

I just found out I'm colour blind. The diagnosis came completely out of the yellow.

If anyone has any fish jokes will they let minnow.

I accidentally left the gas on yesterday and caused an explosion in our house. The wife went through the roof.

This guy knocks on my door and asks me to join the organ donor register. He is a man after my own heart.

I had to close my sandwich business. My partner kept adding twice the amount of fillings. He double cressed me.

If I had a £1 for every time I said something stupid, I'd have £27.54 now.

I've been told I am being left an expensive watch in a distant relative's Will. I hope it's not a wind-up.

My grandfather brought down 23 planes in the Second World War. He was the worst mechanic the Luftwaffe ever had.

I can't find my A-Ha CD anywhere. I've been hunting high and low.

Someone has been messaging me on line asking me to comb my hair, shave and cut my nails. I think I'm being groomed.

My satnav told me to turn around. Now I can't see where I'm going.

A policeman arrived home early one day and caught his wife in bed with three guys. He said, "Hello, Hello, Hello." She said, "What's up? Aren't you talking to me?"

Which knight was always spying on the enemy? Sir Veillance.

Someone just called me, sneezed and hung up. Bloody cold callers.

I saw a plastic surgeon the other day, he looked real to me.

I like a woman who wears beads. You know you can count on her.

I was once told I could get a job as a model. Work for Airfix!

I've been asked for availability to coach football in Sheffield. I told them I can't manage Wednesday.

I remember when plastic surgery was a taboo subject. Nowadays if you mention Botox no-one raises an eyebrow.

My granddad fell into a vat of invisible ink. That was the last I ever saw of him.

The funeral took place today of the man who invented crosswords. He was buried 6 down and 3 across.

I don't do any insect puns. They bug me.

I dated a tennis player once. It didn't work out though. Love meant nothing to her.

I'm exhausted. My meditation CD started skipping, so I've spent the last two hours breathing in.

I have just been attacked by a man on a trampoline. That was some assault.

My Dad always wanted me to be a soldier. But who wants to be a piece of bread and butter?

My pal Jack claims he can communicate with vegetables. Jack and the beans talk.

I was sad to read that the world's clumsiest window cleaner kicked the bucket today.

My Australian friend failed his aboriginal music exam. I asked him, "Did you redo it?"

I don't understand how people get well-known sayings wrong. After all, it's not rocket surgery.

My mate asked me if there was a B&Q in Carmarthen. I told him, "No, but there's four 'L's in Llanelli."

I just saw someone shoplifting from the Disney store. I thought they're taking the mickey.

What position does a ghost play in football? The ghoulie.

I got lost in a jungle once. Luckily I had compass with me. I could thus draw perfect circles with a pencil.

Yesterday my doctor left me in the waiting room for an hour. I thought, 'He can't treat me like this.'

As I get older I think about all the people I lost along the way. Maybe a career as a tour guide wasn't for me.

Statistically, women who carry a little extra weight live longer than men who mention it.

A bike in town keeps running me over. It's a vicious cycle.

I before E except after C disproved by science.

I'm terrified of elevators and I take steps to avoid then.

I ordered a chicken and an egg off the Internet. I wonder which will come first.

Never iron a four leaf clover. You don't want to press your luck.

To whoever stole my copy of Microsoft Office, I will find you – you have my word.

I saw a baguette at the zoo – it was bread in captivity.

My wife said that I snore really badly, so I stayed awake all night to see if she was right.

Why is it that people get simple sayings wrong? Answers on a coastguard please.

I've got an unnatural obsession with feet. I've never accepted the metric system.

My fear of moving stairs is escalating.

The man who fell into an upholstery machine is now fully recovered.

The man who fell into a lens grinding machine made a right spectacle of himself.

I couldn't figure out how to fasten my seat belt. Then it just clicked.

When I had my PlayStation stolen, my family was there to console me.

I was wondering - did anyone find out how much the doggy in the window was?

Alphabetti Spaghetti Bolognese. Pasta for people who like to mince their words.

A boiled egg every morning is hard to beat.

I used to work for a company that made submarines. They went under.

I've finally taught my dog to fetch a glass of red wine. He's a Bordeaux Collie, and yes, he paws it himself.

Someone I know was shot with a starting pistol. Police think it's race-related.

I've finally written my book called 'Growing Beautiful Herbs'. I know, it's about thyme.

I had a club sandwich the other day. I'm not even a member.

The Forestry Commission have announced that it will be shedding jobs this autumn.

I've invented a new portable music system for Bobbies walking the beat. The iPlod.

I've just watched a documentary on how ships are kept together. Riveting.

I've just watched a documentary on how they dig tunnels. Boring.

Capital punishment jokes - they're all about the execution.

I wonder what people who type "u" instead of "you" do with all of their spare time?

I was going to tell you a pizza joke, but it's way too cheesy.

I got my tyres pumped up with air at the local petrol station. Back in the day it was free, then it was 20p, then it was 50p and now it's £1. That's inflation for you.

Don't use a big word, when a simple miniscule semantic expression will adequately achieve the requirement.

If you're being chased by a pack of taxidermists, do not play dead.

I went to see a doctor about my insomnia, but the surgery wasn't open at half past three in the morning.

I always wear a balaclava to bed. That way, if we get burgled during the night, the intruders will think I'm one of their gang.

If a hyena ate an Oxo cube would it make a laughing stock of itself?

Do any of them get found guilty at all those sheep trials?

My optician says I've got 20-20 vision. Oh, sorry, I mis-read that. He says my vision is so-so.

Playground swings - I wouldn't go on one unless I was really pushed.

I staggered into the police station and said, "I've just been attacked by a dwarf in the Red Lion." The copper replied, "We'll get him Sir; he's a gnome troublemaker."

When I told my friends I wanted to start a business selling small pieces of metal, they gave me some flak.

Are sycophants elephants who are unwell?

They say time flies when you are having fun so if you want to live longer, just be miserable.

I've just been invited to join a Tai Chi group. I won't be doing that in a hurry.

My boss was mad at me and yelled, "You really are an ignoramus." I replied, "Why would you call me a dinosaur?"

I caught my dog chewing on a charging cable. I had to ground him. He is doing better currently and conducting himself properly now.

Light switches in the dark. I really feel for them.

They've just opened a new chemists between Specsavers and Greggs in my local town. Yes, it's specs and drugs and sausage rolls.

I've started a boatbuilding business in my garage. Sails are going through the roof.

A waiter in an Icelandic restaurant told me, "We have whale meat, whale meat or the Vera Lynn." I asked him, "What's the Vera Lynn?" He replied, "Whale meat again."

I was going to run five miles on my treadmill, but it's only two metres long.

I stopped having abseiling lessons after the instructor kept letting me down.

The next one wasn't much better – he kept me hanging around.

I've got some toasters to sell; I think I'll open a pop-up shop.

It's all square at the draughtsman's football tournament.

I've been trying to teach my dog how to ride a bicycle, which he's doing really well at, and how to perform classical music, which he's not so good at. His Bach is worse than his bike.

Two blood cells met and fell in love, but it was all in vein.

I looked up cigarette lighters on Google but it came up with 25,000 matches.

My wife asked me why I came home half drunk last night. I told her it was because I ran out of money.

If I catch anyone stealing my stationery to make jewellery, I'll give them a clip around the earhole.

I was in Rome recently and went to see the Spanish Steps. Worst tribute band ever.

My grandfather dies just as he was about to win the Snakes and Ladders World Title. Well at least he was went at the top of his game.

Christie's and Sotheby's - they're really forbidding.

My friend with a lisp has passed away.
He'll be miffed.

Someone rang the doorbell last night and
when I answered it there was a snowman
standing there. Bloody cold callers.

They say football is a game of two halves.
Not for me it isn't. I regularly down eight
or nine pints while watching a live game
in my local.

I've just bought a Neil Diamond
personalised ringtone. It makes a
beautiful noise.

Our puppy has started following my
daughter to Brownies - it wants to be a
Guide dog.

I was once in a band called 'The Prevention', because we hoped people would say we were better than The Cure.

I was once in a band called 'The Radiators'; we were a warm up act.

Then I joined 'The Duvets';we mainly did covers.

I used to be in a group called 'Cats Eyes; mostly middle of the road stuff.

I'm now in a group called 'Missing Cat'; you may have seen our posters.

Tumble driers are so last century. I do all my drying on line.

Magic eye pictures. I don't know what people see in them.

My Labrador Retriever has yet to retrieve a single Labrador.

I used to be a skiing instructor, but my career went downhill.

My mate said he's never going to use a pen again. I said, "Can I have that in writing?"

Why doesn't Head & Shoulders shampoo have a body wash called Knees & Toes?

I don't know much about Switzerland, but I know what their flag looks like, so that's a big plus.

My friends have said I'm not very good at telling jokes, but here goes….. Pick a card, any card.

How do Eskimos keep their houses from falling down? They use I-glue.

I hate clichés, and avoid them like the plague.

If bear grills could grill bears how many bears would bear grills grill ?

Why is 'sunning' yourself OK, but 'mooning' isn't?

At what age is it appropriate to tell my dog he's adopted?

Trying to write with a broken pencil is pointless.

My wife has thrown me out because of my obsession with Arnold Schwarzenegger quotes. I told her, "I'll be back."

My cross-eyed wife and I just got a divorce. I found out she was seeing someone on the side.

I bought my wife a fridge for her birthday. I can't wait to see her face light up when she opens it.

Did you know that 50% of Roger Federer's name is er.

I really believe that the Miss Universe competition is fixed - all the winners are from Earth.

I am struggling to keep up with the youngsters on social media. What does IDK mean?

Do bin men get formal training? Or do they pick it up as they go along?

I just bought a new stick deodorant. It said 'Remove cap and push up bottom.'

I went to see a performance of Beethoven's 9th, and was really disappointed - that big fluffy dog wasn't even in it.

My new girlfriend just called me boring. We'll see about that tomorrow when I show her my train spotting pictures.

I've been charged with not grouping my words together properly. I'm being sentenced tomorrow.

I've put 110% into trying to cure my tendency to exaggerate.

It's really annoying when people call me greedy; as if I haven't already got enough on my plate.

The guy who invented the compass confessed it was the turning point of his career.

It took me four hours to cook some peas yesterday. It said on the tin 'Boil separately.'

I can't seem to get any sleep, I keep worrying about Armageddon; my wife said, "Don't worry dear, it's not the end of the world."

I've just seen a new magic shop on the High Street. It appeared out of nowhere.

Newsagents that don't sell comics have serious issues.

I went to the doctor about having a compulsion to make nasty remarks about people and he prescribed me a course of anti-defamatories.

I've just started up a dating site for chickens. It's not my normal day job; I'm just trying to make hens meet.

My wife said she's leaving me because I think I'm a supermarket cashier. I said, "Do you want any help with your packing?"

It's my wife's birthday next week. She's been leaving jewellery catalogues all over the house, so I've bought her a magazine rack.

I just blocked someone for correcting my grammar and it feelded good.

I was going to bake a wedding cake but knew it would all end in tiers.

Global warming. Is it just hot air?

A Scotsman once told me that the main difference between Robbie Burns and Walt Disney is that Robbie Burns but Walt Disney.

I wonder if you can make a water-bed more bouncy by using spring water.

Kim Kardashian says that bees frighten her. I bet the rest of the alphabet does too.

If anyone wants to come and discuss how bad my DIY skills are, my door's always open.

I just paid £20 for a three mile taxi ride to the launderette. I feel like I've been taken to the cleaners.

This is a terrible time of year to buy a thermometer. They're very high at the moment.

Is gastronomy the science of using a telescope to watch fat people eating?

Every time I try to leave the house my wife blocks the doorway with a wicker basket filled with cakes and jam. She's trying to hamper my progress.

I've written a book; 'Humpty Dumpty - A Bystander's View'. I didn't want to write it, but I was egged on.

My teenage daughter is a n incredibly driven individual. She's always wanting a lift somewhere.

We were so poor when I was a kid that we had normal K for breakfast.

Watching motivational clips on YouTube is my favourite form of procrastination.

I've put all my dogging gear up for sale on eBay. I've not had any bids yet, but there are 7 people watching.

I had a man on my front doorstep for over half an hour telling me about the good things about eating brown bread. Blooming Hovis Witnesses.

Why are the seating areas in a stadium called 'stands'?

When I die, I would like the word 'humble' inscribed on the base of my statue.

They say a camera can add ten pounds, so I've started taking photos of my wallet.

Sheepdog puppies for sale, Come buy.

My mate keeps walking up high mountains in his sleep. I ask myself, will he Everest?

Brighton isn't shaped like a loaf of bread, but Hove is.

On my first day as a supply teacher I took some kids to an outdoor activities centre. When we got there, they started hiding behind trees and another teacher told me they were all a bit backwoods.

Apparently towels are the biggest cause of dry skin.

A cheesy corn puff, an artilleryman and a stripy insect walk into a bar. The barman says, "Wotsit gunner bee?"

I went to mow a meadow earlier accompanied by my dog. Now everyone's at it.

I've got a procrastination joke that I must tell you sometime.

My mate asked me if there was a B&Q in Carmarthen. I told them, "No, but there's four 'L's in Llanelli."

I've just won a box of 6 cricket balls – I was bowled over.

My wife got sent to hospital after swallowing a twenty pound note. There's still no change in her.

My mate is so stupid he thought Sherlock Holmes was a block of apartments.

I've just seen a man at an ATM standing on one leg. I said, "What are you doing?" He replied, "Just checking my balance."

A lorry carrying a delivery of ginger bound for Sainsbury's has overturned on the A1. People are strongly advised to use a different root.

I've quit working in the boiler room. Too much pressure for me.

In a restaurant the other day the waitress shouted "quick, does anyone know CPR?" I replied, "Yes, better than that, I know the whole alphabet." Everyone laughed. Well, except this one guy.

When I'm listening to U2, I turn down the treble a little bit. Just to take The Edge off.

I accidentally sat on a vacuum cleaner accessory. The hospital say they can't get it out, but I'm picking up well.

Children certainly brighten up the home. They never turn the lights off.

I've just been prescribed anti-gloating cream. I can't wait to rub it in.

My Spanish neighbour's young son can't even say 'please'. That's poor for four.

I was in the bank today, where there was an old lady crying with a fiver in her left ear and a tenner in her right ear. The manager said, "She's £15 in arrears."

90% of people are idiots. I'm glad I'm with the other 20%

My local watchmaker died yesterday. He ran out of time.

I've just picked up a rescue cat from Cheshire. Can't stop smiling.

My missus said her grandad was minted. He left her a polo.

Until the day I 'pop my clogs' I'll never understand old sayings.

The first rule of 'Condescending Club' is rather complex and I don't think you'd understand it if I explained it to you.

I'm reading a book about firewood at the moment. It's not on paperback yet - it's only available on kindle.

My wife's not happy with my new job at the cement factory. She thinks I'm mixing with the wrong people.

I'm reading a book on the history of the Hell's Angels. It's good, though there's a lot of chapters.

My friend had to be rushed into hospital after a freak accident left a gyroscope lodged in his head. Doctors describe his condition as very stable.

Magnifying glasses. Are they larger than life?

Have you ever wondered why it is that when you open a tin of evaporated milk, the milk is still there.

If one more person asks me to do a somersault, I swear I'm going to flip.

I've just opened a shop in Jamaica selling glass cookware. It's called Pyrex of the Caribbean.

My mate's pet snake got into my freezer last night. I don't know how to tell him, I reckon I'll have to give it to him straight.

The consumer programme Watchdog has exposed companies selling bogus anti-obesity remedies. The presenter said that these firms had been living off the fat of the land for too long.

My dog's got a job on a building site. He's a roofer.

I met a couple fishing today. They introduced themselves as Rod and Annette.

My girlfriend told me there is a rumour of a new ABBA song. I asked her if Benny wrote it, and she replied, "No, it's Bjorn again."

I've just bought a thesaurus and all the pages are blank. I can't even begin to describe how angry I am.

I have an antique bottle of tippex. It's a correctors item.

I got thrown out of the opera last night. I found out they don't like you joining in.

I had to leave my job at the helium factory. I wasn't going to be spoken to like that.

The stonemason asked to record Rear Of The Year for posterity says he's really hit rock bottom.

When my wife was in labour, the nurse came and said, "What about epidural anaesthesia?" We replied, "We've already picked names."

I used to sell computer parts, but I lost my drive.

Since we bought a waterbed, the wife and I have drifted apart.

I bought some counterfeit Mr Kipling Cakes. I must say they're exceedingly good fakes.

I've just been stung by a bee. Twenty quid for a jar of honey!

I'm writing a book on hurricanes. It's only a draft at the moment.

I've been a bit ill recently, and now I'm on anti-barn dance pills. But I'm not allowed to exceed the dosey dosage.

I used to be a grave robber but I don't like to talk about it. It's just digging up the passed.

My doctor told me I should work out, so I've bought myself a calculator.

I tend to faint at surprises, which is why I lost my job making Kinder Eggs.

I've bought a top of the range Rolls Royce but my budget didn't cover a driver. I've spent all that money and I've got nothing to chauffeur it.

A new world record for a Chinese dumpling has been set. It weighed won ton.

I used to be in a band called Duck's Nostrils. We were always top of the bill.

I just got kicked out of the local clairvoyant society; I should have seen it coming really.

I worked in a barometer factory once. There were highs and lows in the job but I had to leave as there was just too much pressure.

I asked my dad if I was a pyromaniac. He said, "Yes you arson."

Taking the batteries out of my doorbell has had a knock on effect.

My great grandfather survived mustard gas and pepper spray in the First Word War. He was a seasoned veteran.

I'm trying to organise a Hide and Seek tournament, but it's not easy. Good players are hard to find.

There are 10 types of people in this world. Those who understand binary and those who don't.

I did a gig in a fertility clinic. I got a standing ovulation.

My pal Mr Hoover got knocked down crossing the road and has been in hospital for weeks. I went to see him today and he is picking up now.

I got sacked from the bookies yesterday. I said, "Well, it's your loss."

Every time I tell people I'm telekinetic, they strangely move away.

Garden buildings - that's a shed load of timber.

Will glass coffins become a popular trend? Remains to be seen.

My wife wanted something with diamonds in it for our anniversary. So I got her a pack of cards.

My father never did a day's work in his life. He was a night watchman.

I've put 110% into trying to cure my tendency to exaggerate.

I've been on a self-defence course. Now, if I try to self-harm I can protect myself.

I'm not a complete idiot, you know. I have had my appendix removed.

I've just started rolling my own cigarettes. Any tips would be appreciated.

At the age of 65 my grandmother started walking 5 miles a day. She is now 72 and we have no idea where she is.

I had my first cage fight last night. That budgie never knew what hit him.

Did you know they're selling penny whistles in the pound shop.

I used to hate school sports day, I ran a mile.

I took on Dracula in a boxing match. I didn't do very well. I couldn't beat the count.

I've just mended the horn on the boy scout's van. Beep repaired.

My elevator business is up and down all the time.

I've decided not to have kids. The kids aren't taking it too well.

I invented a new type of boxing. You do it on your own. You should try it. Knock yourself out.

I've just deleted all the German names off my phone. Now I'm Hans free.

What goes tick woof, tock woof? A watch dog.

I went to buy some camouflage trousers today, but I couldn't find any.

My doctor has told me I'm morbidly obese. Well he's wrong. I may be fat but I'm not upset about it.

I said to my female doctor, "I think I've got tennis elbow." She said, "How many days have you had that?" I said, "Fifteen love."

The landlord at my pub said that I had won a moped in the pub raffle went to collect it, it was a mop head.

My wife could never get over my obsession with Phil Collins. But take a look at me now.

Is it possible to mistake schizophrenia for telepathy, I hear you ask.

My mate bet me £100 that I couldn't do a butterfly impression. I thought, that's worth a little flutter.

My great grandfather left me half of his estate when he died. Bloody useless - what am I supposed to do with half a car?

I've been told I should be reimbursed for my cancelled snorkelling holiday, but I'm not holding my breath.

After being pestered by fans, David Hasselhoff is changing his name to David Hoff - he can't be bothered with the hassel anymore.

I won't rest until I find a cure for insomnia.

I'm not a good speller, but I'm not the only one. I think those of us who find spelling difficult should get together and form an onion.

Dire Straits and Chris Rea are going to join forces. The new group is going to be called Chris Straits. Much better than the alternative.

I laid awake all night thinking how does the sun come up? Then it dawned on me.

I totally fooled a sheep the other day – I pulled the wool over its eyes.

A yoghurt came up to me and said, "Eat me." It was a proactive yoghurt.

I saw a quiche floating in water. I thought that's flan buoyant.

I went to a fortune teller and asked her if I could have my hand read. She hit it with a hammer.

A psychic got run over by a bus yesterday. He said he didn't see it coming.

Apparently the name Dorothy is common in my family. So, I'm investigating my family tree to see if I can join the dots together.

My wife told me she thinks our marriage is like a pantomime but I told her, "Oh no it isn't."

Apple have offered me a job. Apparently I've got the core values they want.

Did you know Ann Boleyn had a brother called ten pin?

My friend said to me, "Whatever you do don't mention deodorant." I said, "Sure, Mum's the word."

If you are a Hindu woman and you're getting married, would you have a Hindu Hen do?

The wife asked me to bring her something back from Prague. So I got her some check trousers.

A bloke in my pub was selling an LCD TV for a tenner. The only problem is that the volume button doesn't work. Mind you for that price, you can't turn it down.

Orion's belt, now that's a big waist of space.

Acoustic: what a Scottish farmer uses to control his cattle.

Nudists need to be exposed for what they are.

As a rule of thumb, never hit it with a hammer.

I'm useless at Scrabble because my spelling is crop.

I offered the old woman next door £5 for a go on her Stena stair lift. I think she's going to take me up on it.

I was always told to "push the boundaries" when I was growing up. Sadly this was one of the reasons why I got kicked out of the cricket club.

Last night I woke up feeling a little hoarse. That's six nights on the trot now.

I quit my job working for Nike. Just couldn't do it anymore.

My wife asked me to try this new coffee she bought. It was OK, but just not my cup of tea.

I met this story teller who worked for Airfix. He made them up as he went along.

I've just invented a Microwave bed. Now I can get 8 hours sleep in just 4 minutes.

My mate asked me if I preferred dodgems, the waltzer or the helter-skelter. I thought, that's a fair question.

My local football team have signed a locksmith for the upcoming season. I think he'll be a key player.

My partner worked at a factory that made bras but they have just gone bust.

Two goldfish in a tank. One says to the other, "How do you drive this then?"

Every time the doorbell rings, my dog goes and sits in the corner. He's a boxer.

A man with two left feet went into a shoe shop and asked for a pair of flip flips.

I got a new coat for the wife. Best swap I've ever done.

Do copies of the Kama Sutra have flexible spines?

They say a camera can add ten pounds, so I've started taking photos of my wallet.

I just bought stock in some company called Bose. I think it will be a sound investment.

I sneaked into a Spandau Ballet concert. I made it through the barricades.

Even though I've gone bald I still keep the comb I've had for nearly 20 years. I just can't part with it.

I'm always getting 'calendar' and 'colander' mixed up, which is why I find every day a bit of a strain.

I asked the barman if he had any helicopter flavoured crisps. He said, "No, only plane."

I went to the butchers for some tripe. He gave me a Love Island box set.

I was in the record shop and said to the assistant what have you got by the doors? He said some sand and a fire blanket.

Someone has stolen my dictionary. I'm lost for words.

I once had my own business ironing sheets. The customers wanted me to stop ironing so I folded.

A friend of mine had a job ironing fizzy drinks, he gave it up as it was soda pressing.

I used to be obsessed with F1 but now I have moved along the key board.

I visited a prison once, and they said to me watch out for one-eyed Rick. I said, "Why, is he violent?" They replied, "No, he keeps bumping into people."

I'm on anti line dance pills at the moment. I'm not allowed to exceed the dosey dosage.

After a long and distinguished career, the world's foremost paranormal investigator has finally given up the ghost.

My daughter brought her new boyfriend home to meet us. He was in a brilliant white suit, white shoes, even his teeth were bright white. "Hello," he said, "I'm Daz."

The benefit of easy origami is two fold.

What is an occasional table the rest of the time?

I was trying to think of an anagram of 'foolish otters' but then I thought 'life's too short'.

Police have arrested the World Tongue-Twister Champion. I imagine he'll be given a tough sentence.

I'm having a tattoo of the numbers 10 to 1 all down my back today. It's the spinal countdown.

He replied, "Everything comes to him who waits."

Insomnia sufferers – look on the bright side – there are only ten more sleeps until Christmas.

A friend asked me, "Do I like humming birds?" I replied, "mmmmm."

I want to learn how to read music. I keep pronouncing it mussik.

My doctor told me to cut down on starch. He obviously doesn't know how much I hate ironing.

Does anyone know where I can find a decent tie? I've taken four back already because they didn't fit. All too tight.

I once went out with a girl who lived near Loch Ness. It didn't last long though. It was just a Highland fling.

I went to a fancy-dress party as an elephant, but everyone in the room ignored me.

Tequila, schnapps, sambuca. I'm calling the shots.

I've heard of splinters, but I've never seen one in the flesh before.

The collective noun for a group of hayfever sufferers is a choo.

I'm going to France tomorrow for the "Flicking A Ruler On The Edge Of A Desk" championships. It's held annually in the Dordogne.

My friend bought fifty bottles of Tippex from the Internet - I think he has made a big mistake.

I went to the doctors. I said, "When I pass from one country to another I have to get drunk." He said, "You're a borderline alcoholic."

A truck full of Vicks vapour rub has overturned. Traffic is congested.

I got covered in gold paint the other day. I had a bit of a gilt complex.

Why don't polar bears eat penguins? They can't get the wrappers off.

The other day I met the guy who invented crosswords. I can't remember his name. Its p something t something r.

This morning, I woke up laughing. I think I must have slept funny.

This doctor said to this kleptomaniac, take these tablets 3 times a day, if there is no change in a week, get me a big TV and an iPhone.

I've just seen a guy wandering around shouting "Castles." I think he has Turrets Syndrome.

Three cheers for rap music. Hip hop...

I always get emotional at weddings. The last wedding I went to I cried when the vicar said to me, "I'm afraid she hasn't turned up."

My car is unusual – it runs on ferrets. I made the classic mistake this morning. I filled it up with weasels.

Atheism is a non-prophet organisation.

I went to the music shop, and bought a violin. The assistant said, "Do you want a bow as well." I said, "Don't bother wrapping it."

My girlfriend ripped her tights getting into my car, so I gave her my fan belt.

I went to the doctors and I said, "I've got a rash." He said, "I'll be as quick as I can."

My mum had plastic surgery in the 1970s. Sadly she was left with flared nostrils.

Someone threw a bottle of Omega 3 pills at me. Luckily my only injuries were super fish oil.

My Mum is having trouble with her computer. She said, "Whenever I hit this button it swears at me." I said, "Mum that's the cursor."

My wife has just started an admin job in a nail bar. She just does the filing.

I sold my budgie on eBay last week. He went cheap.

I've decided to take up fell-walking in a bid to get fitter. It's going well so far, last night I fell twice walking back from the pub.

Chickens only use 1% of their brains; KFC use the other 99%.

I asked an electrician to fix a wiring issue in my house. He refused.

I hate people that take drugs - Customs Officers, Policemen etc.

Open mike night sounded fun, until I realised I'd been invited to an autopsy.

My favourite word is telephone. I think it's got a nice ring to it.

I said to my father I was going to name my first child after him. Then I thought, actually dad's not a great name for a baby.

I'm a big fan of whiteboards. I find them quite re-markable.

Do you know what I don't understand? Japanese hand writing.

My friend's bakery burnt down yesterday. Now his business is toast.

My girlfriend and I are made for each other. She thinks I'm cute when I don't have my glasses on, and I think she's cute when I don't have my glasses on.

I was burgled last night. They stole all my Custard Creams. That really takes the biscuit.

Sometimes, I question my sanity. The worse thing is, sometimes it replies.

A guy at Dixons asked me, "Do you have a hard drive?" I replied, "No, it's gravel."

My grief counsellor died the other day. Luckily, he was so good I couldn't care less.

I've just been on a positive thinking course. It was rubbish.

My girlfriend thinks everyone laughs at me because I dress up like Adam Ant. I told her ridicule is nothing to be scared of.

I got into a fight with a photographer last night. It was all over in a flash.

Did you hear about the guy whose whole left side was cut off? He's all right now.

A man just assaulted me with milk, cream and butter. How dairy.

I once dated a magazine collector. She had a lot of issues.

I was playing the piano in this bar when this elephant walked in. He started crying his eyes out. I said, "Do you recognise the tune?" He said, "No, I recognise the ivory."

Experience riding a fast horse with the new Giddy App.

If I've learned anything in my 60 years on this planet, it's that it's OK to lie about your age.

Did you hear about those new reversible jackets? I'm excited to see how they turn out.

My female colleague is unable to attend next week's Innuendo Seminar so I will have to fill her slot instead.

Let me know if you want some copies of 'Osteopath's monthly' as I have plenty of back issues.

I asked my solicitor friend if he could help me with my will. He replied, "Sure, leave it to me."

Doctor: "Sir, I'm afraid your DNA is backwards." Patient: "And?"

I'm reading a horror story in Braille. Something bad is about to happen - I can feel it.

I bought some shoes from a drug dealer. I don't know what he laced them with, but I've been tripping all day.

I've just burned 2,000 calories. That's the last time I leave brownies in the oven while I nap.

A plateau is the highest form of flattery.

Thanks for explaining the word "many" to me, it means a lot.

The future, the present and the past walked into a bar. Things got a little tense.

Did you hear about the two silk worms in a race? It ended in a tie.

I asked my French friend if she likes to play video games. She said, "Wii."

Yesterday I accidentally swallowed some food colouring. The doctor says I'm OK, but I feel like I've dyed a little inside.

Becoming a vegetarian is a big missed steak.

Why don't you ever see the headline 'Psychic wins the lottery'?

Did you hear about the man who jumped off a bridge in Paris? He was in Seine.

My girlfriend said, "You act like a detective too much. I want to split up." I replied, "Good idea. We can cover more ground that way."

This morning my alarm went off. I thought its sell-by date was tomorrow.

My neighbour crashed his car into a tree. He now knows how a Mercedes bends.

I'm glad I know sign language. It's pretty handy.

Don't trust atoms, they make up everything.

My friend started a business exporting artificial limbs. He's now an international arms dealer.

There was a right commotion at the local bird sanctuary yesterday. The pheasants were revolting.

When I got as job working on a ghost train, people were surprised.

I was banned from walking my dog Shark along the beach.

I tried to invent a robot gym instructor, but it didn't work out.

I've decided to sell my old Hoover. Well, it was just collecting dust.

I went into a chip shop and said, "Cod and chips twice ." She said, "I heard you the first time."

RIP boiled water. You will be mist.

Trying to write with a broken pencil is pointless.

What is the best thing about living in Switzerland? Well, the flag is a big plus.

I recently heard about a mannequin that lost all of his friends. He was too clothes minded.

Is there always a queue at the snooker club?

Did you hear about the kidnapping at school? It's okay. He woke up.

My girlfriend told me she was leaving me because I keep pretending to be a Transformer. I said, "No, wait, I can change."

Show me a piano falling down a mineshaft and I'll show you A-flat minor.

I had a date last night. I really enjoyed it, so tonight I am going to have a fig.

My ex-wife still misses me. But her aim is steadily improving.

A courtroom artist was arrested today. The details are sketchy.

I can't believe I got fired from the calendar factory. All I did was take a day off.

I'm reading a book about anti-gravity. It's impossible to put down.

I think I remember how I cricked my neck, looking back.

I tell women that I'm available for a limited time only in the hope that their shopping instinct kicks in and they want a bargain.

Hara kiri - it's a dying art.

I went to an imaginary restaurant the other day - CGI Friday's.

As my plane flew through the clouds, I started to get nervous. What if we hit all that data people are storing up here now?

Most people are shocked when they find out how bad an electrician I am.

I wasn't originally going to get a brain transplant, but then I changed my mind.

I have switched the wrappers on my wife's chocolate bars – just to get her snickers in a twix.

I once had a job tying sausages together, but I couldn't make ends meet.

I have bought myself a Feng Shui book. Trouble is I don't know where to put it.

Want to hear a joke about paper? I'm warning you it's tearable.

I used to be addicted to soap. But I'm clean now.

My dad died when we couldn't remember his blood type. As he died, he kept insisting for us to "be positive," but it's hard without him.

A friend of mine tried to annoy me with bird puns, but toucan play at that game.

I once had a job in an orange juice factory, but I got canned. I couldn't concentrate.

A short psychic broke out of jail. It was a small medium at large.

For Halloween we dressed up as almonds. Everyone thought we were nuts.

I lost my mood ring the other day. I'm not sure how to feel about it.

I used to live in a small town in Spain called Macarena. But I don't like to make a song and dance about it.

My wife is leaving me as she thinks I'm obsessed with astronomy. What planet is she on?

A Spanish magician was doing a magic trick. He said, "Uno, dos…" and he then disappeared without a trace.

A truck load of toupees has been stolen. Police are combing the area.

I've written a song about tortillas. Actually, it's more of a rap.

The worst pub I have ever been to was called The Fiddle. It was a vile inn.

About The Author

Chester Croker, known to his friends as Chester the Jester or Croker the Joker, has written many joke books, and has twice been awarded Comedy Writer of the Year by the International Jokers Guild. Chester has met many funny characters in his life that have helped provide him with plenty of material for this book.

If you have seen anything wrong, or have a gag you would like to see included in a future book, please visit the glowwormpress.com website and send a message.

If you enjoyed the book, please review it on Amazon so that others can have a laugh too.

You can also follow Chester on Twitter - @ChesterCroker

The final word:-

I walked into a hotel lobby today. A guy
asked me, "Are you here for the Twitter
conference?" I said, "Yes" so he said,
"Follow me."

I've just finished my first book signing. It
turns out that librarians have no sense of
humour.

Printed in Great Britain
by Amazon